THE BRIEF

PAGES FROM GOD'S STORY

Published by The Scottish Bible Society, Edinburgh

ISBN: 978-0-901518-71-2
2011/10M

Published by:
The Scottish Bible Society
7 Hampton Terrace, Edinburgh EH12 5XU
www.scottishbiblesociety.org

Printed by:
Montgomery Litho Group

THE BRIEF

In 1604 King James VI & I began to fulfil a vision to publish a reliable, readable Bible for the people. He brought together six teams of scholars and gave them the task to faithfully take the words and meaning of the ancient Hebrew and Greek texts and put them into the language of their time. The completed King James Bible, sometimes known as the Authorised Version, was published in 1611.

Four hundred years later our language has changed from that of King James and his translators, making the KJB quite difficult to understand. The Brief is a chance to read some of the KJB again with a contemporary version alongside. Taking short 'brief' sections of the Bible this mini book gives an overview of the bigger Bible story and its themes.

The headings on each page are not direct quotes from the Bible but are there as a guide for today's reader.

THE FIRST DAY

In the beginning God created the heaven and the earth.

And the earth was without form, and void; and darkness was upon the face of the deep. And the Spirit of God moved upon the face of the waters.

And God said, Let there be light: and there was light.

And God saw the light, that it was good: and God divided the light from the darkness.

And God called the light Day, and the darkness he called Night. And the evening and the morning were the first day.

Taken from the book of Genesis, chapter one

THE FIRST DAY

In the beginning God created the heavens and the earth. The earth was formless and empty, and darkness covered the deep waters. And the Spirit of God was hovering over the surface of the waters.

Then God said, "Let there be light," and there was light. And God saw that the light was good. Then he separated the light from the darkness. God called the light "day" and the darkness "night."

And evening passed and morning came, marking the first day.

Taken from the book of Genesis, chapter one

THE FIRST MAN

And God said, Let us make man in our image, after our likeness: and let them have dominion over the fish of the sea, and over the fowl of the air, and over the cattle, and over all the earth, and over every creeping thing that creepeth upon the earth.

So God created man in his own image, in the image of God created he him; male and female created he them.

And the LORD God said, It is not good that the man should be alone; I will make him an help meet for him.

And out of the ground the LORD God formed every beast of the field, and every fowl of the air; and brought them unto Adam to see what he would call them: and whatsoever Adam called every living creature, that was the name thereof.

And Adam gave names to all cattle, and to the fowl of the air, and to every beast of the field; but for Adam there was not found an help meet for him.

Taken from the book of Genesis, chapters one and two

THE FIRST MAN

Then God said, "Let us make human beings in our image, to be like us. They will reign over the fish in the sea, the birds in the sky, the livestock, all the wild animals on the earth, and the small animals that scurry along the ground."

So God created human beings in his own image.
In the image of God he created them;
male and female he created them.

Then the LORD God said, "It is not good for the man to be alone. I will make a helper who is just right for him." So the LORD God formed from the ground all the wild animals and all the birds of the sky. He brought them to the man to see what he would call them, and the man chose a name for each one. He gave names to all the livestock, all the birds of the sky, and all the wild animals. But still there was no helper just right for him.

Taken from the book of Genesis, chapters one and two

THE FIRST PARTNER

And the LORD God caused a deep sleep to fall upon Adam, and he slept: and he took one of his ribs, and closed up the flesh instead thereof;

And the rib, which the LORD God had taken from man, made he a woman, and brought her unto the man.

And Adam said, This is now bone of my bones, and flesh of my flesh: she shall be called Woman, because she was taken out of Man.

Therefore shall a man leave his father and his mother, and shall cleave unto his wife: and they shall be one flesh.

And they were both naked, the man and his wife, and were not ashamed.

Taken from the book of Genesis, chapter two

THE FIRST PARTNER

So the LORD God caused the man to fall into a deep sleep. While the man slept, the LORD God took out one of the man's ribs and closed up the opening. Then the LORD God made a woman from the rib, and he brought her to the man.

"At last!" the man exclaimed.
"This one is bone from my bone,
and flesh from my flesh!
She will be called 'woman,'
because she was taken from 'man.'"

This explains why a man leaves his father and mother and is joined to his wife, and the two are united into one.

Now the man and his wife were both naked, but they felt no shame.

Taken from the book of Genesis, chapter two

THE FIRST EXCUSE

And they heard the voice of the LORD God walking in the garden in the cool of the day: and Adam and his wife hid themselves from the presence of the LORD God amongst the trees of the garden.

And the LORD God called unto Adam, and said unto him, where art thou? And he said, I heard thy voice in the garden, and I was afraid, because I was naked; and I hid myself. And he said, who told thee that thou wast naked? Hast thou eaten of the tree, whereof I commanded thee that thou shouldest not eat?

And the man said, the woman whom thou gavest to be with me, she gave me of the tree, and I did eat. And the LORD God said unto the woman, what is this that thou hast done? And the woman said, the serpent beguiled me, and I did eat.

Taken from the book of Genesis, chapter three

THE FIRST EXCUSE

When the cool evening breezes were blowing, the man and his wife heard the LORD God walking about in the garden. So they hid from the LORD God among the trees. Then the LORD God called to the man, "Where are you?"

He replied, "I heard you walking in the garden, so I hid. I was afraid because I was naked." "Who told you that you were naked?" the LORD God asked. "Have you eaten from the tree whose fruit I commanded you not to eat?" The man replied, "It was the woman you gave me who gave me the fruit, and I ate it."

Then the LORD God asked the woman, "What have you done?" "The serpent deceived me," she replied. "That's why I ate it."

Taken from the book of Genesis, chapter three

THE FIRST SEPARATION

And the LORD God said, Behold, the man is become as one of us, to know good and evil: and now, lest he put forth his hand, and take also of the tree of life, and eat, and live forever:

Therefore the LORD God sent him forth from the Garden of Eden, to till the ground from whence he was taken.

So he drove out the man; and he placed at the east of the garden of Eden Cherubims, and a flaming sword which turned every way, to keep the way of the tree of life.

Taken from the book of Genesis, chapter three

THE FIRST SEPARATION

Then the LORD God said, "Look, the human beings have become like us, knowing both good and evil. What if they reach out, take fruit from the tree of life, and eat it? Then they will live forever!" So the LORD God banished them from the Garden of Eden, and he sent Adam out to cultivate the ground from which he had been made. After sending them out, the LORD God stationed mighty cherubim to the east of the Garden of Eden. And he placed a flaming sword that flashed back and forth to guard the way to the tree of life.

Taken from the book of Genesis, chapter three

THE FIRST PROMISE

And God said, this is the token of the covenant which I make between me and you and every living creature that is with you, for perpetual generations...

I do set my bow in the cloud, and it shall be for a token of a covenant between me and the earth. And it shall come to pass, when I bring a cloud over the earth, that the bow shall be seen in the cloud:

And I will remember my covenant, which is between me and you and every living creature of all flesh...

Taken from the book of Genesis, chapter nine

THE FIRST PROMISE

Then God said, "I am giving you a sign of my covenant with you and with all living creatures, for all generations to come. I have placed my rainbow in the clouds. It is the sign of my covenant with you and with all the earth. When I send clouds over the earth, the rainbow will appear in the clouds and I will remember my covenant with you and with all living creatures."

Taken from the book of Genesis, chapter nine

After this, God continued to speak with people through succeeding generations. One day he spoke to a man called Abraham, calling him to go to a land that God would show him. God promised that through him, God would create a great nation. And so it was that through Abraham, his son Isaac and his grandson Jacob, the Israelite nation grew in great numbers...

Then while they were slaves in Egypt [a long story] God provided them with a great leader called Moses, who rescued them from their miserable life and took them on a journey to what God called 'the promised land'! Their wandering through the Sinai desert was mainly a bitter and painful experience and took them 40 years! It was while they were on the way that God gave them some words as guidance for living together in community.

We call them the Ten Commandments.

THE TEN

And God spake all these words, saying, Thou shalt have no other gods before me. Thou shalt not make unto thee any graven image, or any likeness of anything that is in heaven above, or that is in the earth beneath, or that is in the water under the earth.

Thou shalt not bow down thyself to them, nor serve them: for I the LORD thy God am a jealous God, visiting the iniquity of the fathers upon the children unto the third and fourth generation of them that hate me; And shewing mercy unto thousands of them that love me, and keep my commandments.

Thou shalt not take the name of the LORD thy God in vain; for the LORD will not hold him guiltless that taketh his name in vain. Remember the sabbath day, to keep it holy. Six days shalt thou labour, and do all thy work: But the seventh day is the sabbath of the LORD thy God: in it thou shalt not do any work, thou, nor thy son, nor thy daughter, thy manservant, nor thy maidservant, nor thy cattle, nor thy stranger that is within thy gates: For in six days the LORD made heaven and earth, the sea, and all that in them is, and rested the seventh day: wherefore the LORD blessed the sabbath day, and hallowed it.

Honour thy father and thy mother: that thy days may be long upon the land which the LORD thy God giveth thee. Thou shalt not kill. Thou shalt not commit adultery. Thou shalt not steal. Thou shalt not bear false witness against thy neighbour. Thou shalt not covet thy neighbour's house, thou shalt not covet thy neighbour's wife, nor his manservant, nor his maidservant, nor his ox, nor his ass, nor any thing that is thy neighbour's.

Taken from the book of Exodus, chapters nineteen and twenty

THE TEN

Then God gave the people all these instructions...

"You must not have any other god but me.

"You must not make for yourself an idol of any kind or an image of anything in the heavens or on the earth or in the sea. You must not bow down to them or worship them, for I, the LORD your God, am a jealous God who will not tolerate your affection for any other gods. I lay the sins of the parents upon their children; the entire family is affected—even children in the third and fourth generations of those who reject me. But I lavish unfailing love for a thousand generations on those who love me and obey my commands.

"You must not misuse the name of the LORD your God. The LORD will not let you go unpunished if you misuse his name. Remember to observe the Sabbath day by keeping it holy. You have six days each week for your ordinary work, but the seventh day is a Sabbath day of rest dedicated to the LORD your God. On that day no one in your household may do any work. This includes you, your sons and daughters, your male and female servants, your livestock, and any foreigners living among you. For in six days the LORD made the heavens, the earth, the sea, and everything in them; but on the seventh day he rested. That is why the LORD blessed the Sabbath day and set it apart as holy.

"Honor your father and mother. Then you will live a long, full life in the land the LORD your God is giving you. You must not murder. You must not commit adultery. You must not steal. You must not testify falsely against your neighbor. You must not covet your neighbor's house. You must not covet your neighbor's wife, male or female servant, ox or donkey, or anything else that belongs to your neighbor."

Taken from the book of Exodus, chapters nineteen and twenty

THE REBELLION

And when the people saw that Moses delayed to come down out of the mount, the people gathered themselves together unto Aaron, and said unto him, Up, make us gods, which shall go before us; for as for this Moses, the man that brought us up out of the land of Egypt, we wot not what is become of him.

And Aaron said unto them, Break off the golden earrings, which are in the ears of your wives, of your sons, and of your daughters, and bring them unto me. And all the people brake off the golden earrings which were in their ears, and brought them unto Aaron. And he received them at their hand, and fashioned it with a graving tool, after he had made it a molten calf: and they said, These be thy gods, O Israel, which brought thee up out of the land of Egypt.

And when Aaron saw it, he built an altar before it; and Aaron made proclamation, and said, Tomorrow is a feast to the LORD. And they rose up early on the morrow, and offered burnt offerings, and brought peace offerings; and the people sat down to eat and to drink, and rose up to play.

And the LORD said unto Moses, Go, get thee down; for thy people, which thou broughtest out of the land of Egypt, have corrupted themselves: They have turned aside quickly out of the way which I commanded them: they have made them a molten calf, and have worshipped it, and have sacrificed thereunto, and said, These be thy gods, O Israel, which have brought thee up out of the land of Egypt.

Taken from the book of Exodus, chapter thirty-two

THE REBELLION

When the people saw how long it was taking Moses to come back down the mountain, they gathered around Aaron. "Come on," they said, "make us some gods who can lead us. We don't know what happened to this fellow Moses, who brought us here from the land of Egypt."

So Aaron said, "Take the gold rings from the ears of your wives and sons and daughters, and bring them to me." All the people took the gold rings from their ears and brought them to Aaron. Then Aaron took the gold, melted it down, and molded it into the shape of a calf. When the people saw it, they exclaimed, "O Israel, these are the gods who brought you out of the land of Egypt!"

Aaron saw how excited the people were, so he built an altar in front of the calf. Then he announced, "Tomorrow will be a festival to the LORD!" The people got up early the next morning to sacrifice burnt offerings and peace offerings. After this, they celebrated with feasting and drinking, and they indulged in pagan revelry.

The LORD told Moses, "Quick! Go down the mountain! Your people whom you brought from the land of Egypt have corrupted themselves. How quickly they have turned away from the way I commanded them to live! They have melted down gold and made a calf, and they have bowed down and sacrificed to it. They are saying, 'These are your gods, O Israel, who brought you out of the land of Egypt.'"

Taken from the book of Exodus, chapter thirty-two

THE AFTERMATH

And Moses said unto Aaron, What did this people unto thee, that thou hast brought so great a sin upon them?

And Aaron said, Let not the anger of my LORD wax hot: thou knowest the people, that they are set on mischief.

For they said unto me, Make us gods, which shall go before us: for as for this Moses, the man that brought us up out of the land of Egypt, we wot not what is become of him.

And I said unto them, Whosoever hath any gold, let them break it off. So they gave it me: then I cast it into the fire, and there came out this calf.

For the LORD had said unto Moses, Say unto the children of Israel, Ye are a stiffnecked people.

Taken from the book of Exodus, chapters thirty-two and thirty-three

THE AFTERMATH

Finally, he turned to Aaron and demanded, "What did these people do to you to make you bring such terrible sin upon them?"

"Don't get so upset, my LORD," Aaron replied. "You yourself know how evil these people are. They said to me, 'Make us gods who will lead us. We don't know what happened to this fellow Moses, who brought us here from the land of Egypt.' So I told them, 'Whoever has gold jewelry, take it off.' When they brought it to me, I simply threw it into the fire—and out came this calf!"

For the LORD had told Moses to tell them, "You are a stubborn and rebellious people."

Taken from the book of Exodus, chapters thirty-two and thirty-three

THE WALK

Blessed is the man that walketh not in the counsel of the ungodly, nor standeth in the way of sinners, nor sitteth in the seat of the scornful.

But his delight is in the law of the LORD; and in his law doth he meditate day and night.

And he shall be like a tree planted by the rivers of water, that bringeth forth his fruit in his season; his leaf also shall not wither; and whatsoever he doeth shall prosper.

Taken from the book of Psalms, number one

THE WALK

Oh, the joys of those who do not follow the advice of the wicked, or stand around with sinners, or join in with mockers.

But they delight in the law of the LORD, meditating on it day and night.

They are like trees planted along the riverbank, bearing fruit each season.

Their leaves never wither and they prosper in all they do.

Taken from the book of Psalms, number one

THE SHEPHERD

The LORD is my shepherd; I shall not want.

He maketh me to lie down in green pastures: he leadeth me beside the still waters.

He restoreth my soul: he leadeth me in the paths of righteousness for his name's sake.

Yea, though I walk through the valley of the shadow of death, I will fear no evil: for thou art with me; thy rod and thy staff they comfort me.

Thou preparest a table before me in the presence of mine enemies: thou anointest my head with oil; my cup runneth over.

Surely goodness and mercy shall follow me all the days of my life: and I will dwell in the house of the LORD forever.

Taken from the book of Psalms, number twenty-three

THE SHEPHERD

The LORD is my shepherd; I have all that I need.

He lets me rest in green meadows; he leads me beside peaceful streams. He renews my strength.

He guides me along right paths, bringing honor to his name.

Even when I walk through the darkest valley,
I will not be afraid, for you are close beside me.

Your rod and your staff protect and comfort me.

You prepare a feast for me in the presence of my enemies.

You honor me by anointing my head with oil. My cup overflows with blessings.

Surely your goodness and unfailing love will pursue me
all the days of my life,
and I will live in the house of the LORD forever.

Taken from the book of Psalms, number twenty-three

THE EXILE

By the rivers of Babylon, there we sat down, yea, we wept, when we remembered Zion.

We hanged our harps upon the willows in the midst thereof.

For there they that carried us away captive required of us a song; and they that wasted us required of us mirth, saying, Sing us one of the songs of Zion.

How shall we sing the LORD's song in a strange land?

Taken from the book of Psalms, number one hundred and thirty-seven

THE EXILE

Beside the rivers of Babylon, we sat and wept as we thought of Jerusalem.

We put away our harps, hanging them on the branches of poplar trees.

For our captors demanded a song from us. Our tormentors insisted on a joyful hymn:
"Sing us one of those songs of Jerusalem!"

But how can we sing the songs of the LORD while in a pagan land?

Taken from the book of Psalms, number one hundred and thirty-seven

THE MAN

He is despised and rejected of men; a man of sorrows, and acquainted with grief: and we hid as it were our faces from him; he was despised, and we esteemed him not.

Surely he hath borne our griefs, and carried our sorrows: yet we did esteem him stricken, smitten of God, and afflicted.

But he was wounded for our transgressions, he was bruised for our iniquities: the chastisement of our peace was upon him; and with his stripes we are healed.

All we like sheep have gone astray; we have turned everyone to his own way; and the LORD hath laid on him the iniquity of us all.

Taken from the book of Isaiah, chapter fifty-three

THE MAN

He was despised and rejected—a man of sorrows, acquainted with deepest grief. We turned our backs on him and looked the other way. He was despised, and we did not care.

Yet it was our weaknesses he carried; it was our sorrows that weighed him down. And we thought his troubles were a punishment from God, a punishment for his own sins! But he was pierced for our rebellion, crushed for our sins. He was beaten so we could be whole. He was whipped so we could be healed.

All of us, like sheep, have strayed away.

We have left God's paths to follow our own.

Yet the LORD laid on him the sins of us all.

Taken from the book of Isaiah, chapter fifty-three

THE LORD'S SONG

Praise ye the LORD. Praise God in his sanctuary: praise him in the firmament of his power.

Praise him for his mighty acts: praise him according to his excellent greatness.

Praise him with the sound of the trumpet: praise him with the psaltery and harp.

Praise him with the timbrel and dance: praise him with stringed instruments and organs.

Praise him upon the loud cymbals: praise him upon the high sounding cymbals.

Let everything that hath breath praise the LORD.

Praise ye the LORD.

Taken from the book of Psalms, number one hundred and fifty

THE LORD'S SONG

Praise the LORD!

Praise God in his sanctuary; praise him in his mighty heaven! Praise him for his mighty works; praise his unequaled greatness!

Praise him with a blast of the ram's horn; praise him with the lyre and harp!

Praise him with the tambourine and dancing; praise him with strings and flutes!

Praise him with a clash of cymbals; praise him with loud clanging cymbals.

Let everything that breathes sing praises to the LORD!

Praise the LORD!

Taken from the book of Psalms, number one hundred and fifty

THE PROPHECY

For unto us a child is born, unto us a son is given: and the government shall be upon his shoulder: and his name shall be called Wonderful, Counsellor, The mighty God, The everlasting Father, The Prince of Peace.

Taken from the book of Isaiah, chapter nine

THE PROPHECY

For a child is born to us, a son is given to us.
The government will rest on his shoulders.
And he will be called: Wonderful Counselor, Mighty God,
Everlasting Father, Prince of Peace.

Taken from the book of Isaiah, chapter nine

WORD

In the beginning was the Word, and the Word was with God, and the Word was God.

The same was in the beginning with God.

All things were made by him; and without him was not anything made that was made.

In him was life; and the life was the light of men.

And the light shineth in darkness; and the darkness comprehended it not.

Taken from the Gospel of John, chapter one

WORD

In the beginning the Word already existed.

The Word was with God and the Word was God.

He existed in the beginning with God. God created everything through him and nothing was created except through him.

The Word gave life to everything that was created and his life brought light to everyone.

The light shines in the darkness and the darkness can never extinguish it.

Taken from the Gospel of John, chapter one

BOY

And so it was, that, while they were there, the days were accomplished that she should be delivered.

And she brought forth her firstborn son, and wrapped him in swaddling clothes, and laid him in a manger; because there was no room for them in the inn.

Taken from the Gospel of Luke, chapter two

BOY

And while they were there, the time came for her baby to be born. She gave birth to her first child, a son. She wrapped him snugly in strips of cloth and laid him in a manger, because there was no lodging available for them.

Taken from the Gospel of Luke, chapter two

SON

And it came to pass in those days that Jesus came from Nazareth of Galilee, and was baptized of John in Jordan.

And straightway coming up out of the water, he saw the heavens opened, and the Spirit like a dove descending upon him:

And there came a voice from heaven, saying, Thou art my beloved Son, in whom I am well pleased.

Taken from the Gospel of Mark, chapter one

SON

One day Jesus came from Nazareth in Galilee, and John baptized him in the Jordan River. As Jesus came up out of the water, he saw the heavens splitting apart and the Holy Spirit descending on him like a dove. And a voice from heaven said, "You are my dearly loved Son, and you bring me great joy."

Taken from the Gospel of Mark, chapter one

MAN

And Jesus being full of the Holy Ghost returned from Jordan, and was led by the Spirit into the wilderness,

Being forty days tempted of the devil. And in those days he did eat nothing: and when they were ended, he afterward hungered.

And the devil said unto him, If thou be the Son of God command this stone that it be made bread.

And Jesus answered him, saying, It is written, That man shall not live by bread alone, but by every word of God.

Taken from the Gospel of Luke, chapter four

MAN

Then Jesus, full of the Holy Spirit, returned from the Jordan River. He was led by the Spirit in the wilderness, where he was tempted by the devil for forty days. Jesus ate nothing all that time and became very hungry.

Then the devil said to him, "If you are the Son of God, tell this stone to become a loaf of bread."

But Jesus told him, "No! The Scriptures say, 'People do not live by bread alone.'"

Taken from the Gospel of Luke, chapter four

TEACHER

And a certain ruler asked him, saying, Good Master, what shall I do to inherit eternal life?

And Jesus said unto him, Why callest thou me good? None is good, save one, that is, God.

Taken from the Gospel of Luke, chapter eighteen

TEACHER

Once a religious leader asked Jesus this question: "Good Teacher, what should I do to inherit eternal life?"

"Why do you call me good?" Jesus asked him. "Only God is truly good."

Taken from the Gospel of Luke, chapter eighteen

BLESSINGS

Blessed are the poor in spirit: for theirs is the kingdom of heaven

Blessed are they that mourn: for they shall be comforted.

Blessed are the meek: for they shall inherit the earth.

Blessed are they which do hunger and thirst after righteousness: for they shall be filled.

Blessed are the merciful: for they shall obtain mercy.

Blessed are the pure in heart: for they shall see God.

Blessed are the peacemakers: for they shall be called the children of God.

Taken from the Gospel of Matthew, chapter five

BLESSINGS

"God blesses those who are poor and realize their need for him, for the Kingdom of Heaven is theirs.

God blesses those who mourn, for they will be comforted.

God blesses those who are humble, for they will inherit the whole earth.

God blesses those who hunger and thirst for justice, for they will be satisfied.

God blesses those who are merciful, for they will be shown mercy.

God blesses those whose hearts are pure, for they will see God.

God blesses those who work for peace, for they will be called the children of God."

Taken from the Gospel of Matthew, chapter five

TOUCH

And when Jesus departed thence, two blind men followed him, crying, and saying, Thou son of David, have mercy on us.

And when he was come into the house, the blind men came to him: and Jesus saith unto them, Believe ye that I am able to do this?

They said unto him, Yea, Lord.

Then touched he their eyes, saying, According to your faith be it unto you.

And their eyes were opened...

Taken from the Gospel of Matthew, chapter nine

TOUCH

After Jesus left ... two blind men followed along behind him, shouting, "Son of David, have mercy on us!"

They went right into the house where he was staying, and Jesus asked them, "Do you believe I can make you see?"

"Yes, Lord," they told him, "we do."

Then he touched their eyes and said, "Because of your faith, it will happen."

Then their eyes were opened...

Taken from the Gospel of Matthew, chapter nine

LOST

And he said, A certain man had two sons: and the younger of them said to his father, Father, give me the portion of goods that falleth to me. And he divided unto them his living.

And not many days after, the younger son gathered all together and took his journey into a far country and there wasted his substance with riotous living.

And when he had spent all, there arose a mighty famine in that land; and he began to be in want. And he went and joined himself to a citizen of that country; and he sent him into his fields to feed swine. And he would fain have filled his belly with the husks that the swine did eat: and no man gave unto him.

And when he came to himself, he said, How many hired servants of my father's have bread enough and to spare, and I perish with hunger! I will arise and go to my father, and will say unto him, Father, I have sinned against heaven, and before thee, and am no more worthy to be called thy son: make me as one of thy hired servants.

And he arose, and came to his father. But when he was yet a great way off, his father saw him and had compassion, and ran, and fell on his neck, and kissed him.

Taken from the Gospel of Luke, chapter fifteen

LOST

To illustrate the point further, Jesus told them this story: "A man had two sons. The younger son told his father, 'I want my share of your estate now before you die.' So his father agreed to divide his wealth between his sons.

"A few days later this younger son packed all his belongings and moved to a distant land, and there he wasted all his money in wild living. About the time his money ran out, a great famine swept over the land, and he began to starve. He persuaded a local farmer to hire him, and the man sent him into his fields to feed the pigs. The young man became so hungry that even the pods he was feeding the pigs looked good to him. But no one gave him anything.

"When he finally came to his senses, he said to himself, 'At home even the hired servants have food enough to spare, and here I am dying of hunger! I will go home to my father and say, "Father, I have sinned against both heaven and you and I am no longer worthy of being called your son. Please take me on as a hired servant."'

"So he returned home to his father. And while he was still a long way off, his father saw him coming. Filled with love and compassion, he ran to his son, embraced him, and kissed him."

Taken from the Gospel of Luke, chapter fifteen

FOUND

And the son said unto him, Father, I have sinned against heaven, and in thy sight, and am no more worthy to be called thy son.

But the father said to his servants, Bring forth the best robe, and put it on him; and put a ring on his hand, and shoes on his feet:

And bring hither the fatted calf, and kill it; and let us eat, and be merry:

For this my son was dead, and is alive again; he was lost, and is found. And they began to be merry.

Taken from the Gospel of Luke, chapter fifteen

FOUND

"His son said to him, 'Father, I have sinned against both heaven and you, and I am no longer worthy of being called your son.'

"But his father said to the servants, 'Quick! Bring the finest robe in the house and put it on him. Get a ring for his finger and sandals for his feet. And kill the calf we have been fattening. We must celebrate with a feast, for this son of mine was dead and has now returned to life. He was lost, but now he is found.' So the party began."

Taken from the Gospel of Luke, chapter fifteen

GRIEF

Then when Mary was come where Jesus was, and saw him, she fell down at his feet, saying unto him, Lord, if thou hadst been here, my brother had not died.

When Jesus therefore saw her weeping, and the Jews also weeping which came with her, he groaned in the spirit, and was troubled.

And said, Where have ye laid him? They said unto him, Lord, come and see.

Jesus wept.

Taken from the Gospel of John, chapter eleven

GRIEF

When Mary arrived and saw Jesus, she fell at his feet and said, "Lord, if only you had been here, my brother would not have died."

When Jesus saw her weeping and saw the other people wailing with her, a deep anger welled up within him and he was deeply troubled.

"Where have you put him?" he asked them. They told him, "Lord, come and see."

Then Jesus wept.

Taken from the Gospel of John, chapter eleven

JOY

Jesus said, Take ye away the stone. Martha, the sister of him that was dead, saith unto him, LORD, by this time he stinketh: for he hath been dead four days. Jesus saith unto her, Said I not unto thee, that, if thou wouldest believe, thou shouldest see the glory of God?

Then they took away the stone from the place where the dead was laid. And Jesus lifted up his eyes, and said, Father, I thank thee that thou hast heard me. And I knew that thou hearest me always: but because of the people which stand by I said it, that they may believe that thou hast sent me.

And when he thus had spoken, he cried with a loud voice, Lazarus, come forth.

And he that was dead came forth, bound hand and foot with graveclothes: and his face was bound about with a napkin. Jesus saith unto them, Loose him, and let him go.

Taken from the Gospel of John, chapter eleven

JOY

"Roll the stone aside," Jesus told them.

But Martha, the dead man's sister, protested, "Lord, he has been dead for four days. The smell will be terrible."

Jesus responded, "Didn't I tell you that you would see God's glory if you believe?" So they rolled the stone aside. Then Jesus looked up to heaven and said, "Father, thank you for hearing me. You always hear me, but I said it out loud for the sake of all these people standing here, so that they will believe you sent me."

Then Jesus shouted, "Lazarus, come out!" And the dead man came out, his hands and feet bound in grave clothes, his face wrapped in a head cloth. Jesus told them, "Unwrap him and let him go!"

Taken from the Gospel of John, chapter eleven

LOVE

For God so loved the world, that he gave his only begotten Son, that whosoever believeth in him should not perish, but have everlasting life.

For God sent not his Son into the world to condemn the world; but that the world through him might be saved.

Taken from the Gospel of John, chapter three

LOVE

"For God loved the world so much that he gave his one and only Son, so that everyone who believes in him will not perish but have eternal life. God sent his Son into the world not to judge the world, but to save the world through him."

Taken from the Gospel of John, chapter three

BETRAYAL

And he took bread, and gave thanks, and brake it, and gave unto them, saying, This is my body which is given for you: this do in remembrance of me.

Likewise also the cup after supper, saying, This cup is the new testament in my blood, which is shed for you.

But, behold, the hand of him that betrayeth me is with me on the table.

Taken from the Gospel of Luke, chapter twenty-two

BETRAYAL

He took some bread and gave thanks to God for it. Then he broke it in pieces and gave it to the disciples, saying, "This is my body, which is given for you. Do this to remember me."

After supper he took another cup of wine and said, "This cup is the new covenant between God and his people—an agreement confirmed with my blood, which is poured out as a sacrifice for you.

"But here at this table, sitting among us as a friend, is the man who will betray me."

Taken from the Gospel of Luke, chapter twenty-two

AGONY

And he came out, and went, as he was wont, to the mount of Olives; and his disciples also followed him.

And when he was at the place, he said unto them, Pray that ye enter not into temptation.

And he was withdrawn from them about a stone's cast, and kneeled down, and prayed,

Saying, Father, if thou be willing, remove this cup from me: nevertheless not my will, but thine, be done.

And there appeared an angel unto him from heaven, strengthening him.

And being in an agony he prayed more earnestly: and his sweat was as it were great drops of blood falling down to the ground.

Taken from the Gospel of Luke, chapter twenty-two

AGONY

Then, accompanied by the disciples, Jesus left the upstairs room and went as usual to the Mount of Olives. There he told them, "Pray that you will not give in to temptation."

He walked away, about a stone's throw, and knelt down and prayed, "Father, if you are willing, please take this cup of suffering away from me. Yet I want your will to be done, not mine." Then an angel from heaven appeared and strengthened him. He prayed more fervently, and he was in such agony of spirit that his sweat fell to the ground like great drops of blood.

Taken from the Gospel of Luke, chapter twenty-two

KING

And the whole multitude of them arose, and led him unto Pilate.

And they began to accuse him, saying, We found this fellow perverting the nation, and forbidding to give tribute to Caesar, saying that he himself is Christ a King.

And Pilate asked him, saying, Art thou the King of the Jews? And he answered him and said, Thou sayest it.

Taken from the Gospel of Luke, chapter twenty-three

KING

Then the entire council took Jesus to Pilate, the Roman governor. They began to state their case: "This man has been leading our people astray by telling them not to pay their taxes to the Roman government and by claiming he is the Messiah, a king."

So Pilate asked him, "Are you the king of the Jews?"

Jesus replied, "You have said it."

Taken from the Gospel of Luke, chapter twenty-three

MOB

Pilate therefore, willing to release Jesus, spake again to them.

But they cried, saying, Crucify him, crucify him.

And he said unto them the third time, Why, what evil hath he done?

Taken from the Gospel of Luke, chapter twenty-three

MOB

Pilate argued with them, because he wanted to release Jesus. But they kept shouting, "Crucify him! Crucify him!"

For the third time he demanded, "Why? What crime has he committed?"

Taken from the Gospel of Luke, chapter twenty-three

PLACE

And there were also two other, malefactors, led with him to be put to death.

And when they were come to the place, which is called Calvary, there they crucified him, and the malefactors, one on the right hand, and the other on the left.

Then said Jesus, Father, forgive them; for they know not what they do.

Taken from the Gospel of Luke, chapter twenty-three

PLACE

Two others, both criminals, were led out to be executed with him. When they came to a place called The Skull, they nailed him to the cross. And the criminals were also crucified—one on his right and one on his left.

Jesus said, "Father, forgive them, for they don't know what they are doing."

Taken from the Gospel of Luke, chapter twenty-three

PARADISE

THIS IS THE KING OF THE JEWS.

And one of the malefactors which were hanged railed on him, saying, If thou be Christ, save thyself and us.

But the other answering rebuked him, saying, Dost not thou fear God, seeing thou art in the same condemnation?

And we indeed justly; for we receive the due reward of our deeds: but this man hath done nothing amiss.

And he said unto Jesus, Lord, remember me when thou comest into thy kingdom.

And Jesus said unto him, Verily I say unto thee, Today shalt thou be with me in paradise.

Taken from the Gospel of Luke, chapter twenty-three

PARADISE

"This is the King of the Jews."

One of the criminals hanging beside him scoffed, "So you're the Messiah, are you? Prove it by saving yourself—and us, too, while you're at it!"

But the other criminal protested, "Don't you fear God even when you have been sentenced to die? We deserve to die for our crimes, but this man hasn't done anything wrong." Then he said, "Jesus, remember me when you come into your Kingdom."

And Jesus replied, "I assure you, today you will be with me in paradise."

Taken from the Gospel of Luke, chapter twenty-three

DEATH

And it was about the sixth hour, and there was a darkness over all the earth until the ninth hour.

And the sun was darkened, and the veil of the temple was rent in the midst.

And when Jesus had cried with a loud voice, he said, Father, into thy hands I commend my spirit: and having said thus, he gave up the ghost.

Taken from the Gospel of Luke, chapter twenty-three

DEATH

By this time it was noon, and darkness fell across the whole land until three o'clock. The light from the sun was gone. And suddenly, the curtain in the sanctuary of the Temple was torn down the middle. Then Jesus shouted, "Father, I entrust my spirit into your hands!" And with those words he breathed his last.

Taken from the Gospel of Luke, chapter twenty-three

LIFE

Now upon the first day of the week, very early in the morning, they came unto the sepulchre, bringing the spices which they had prepared, and certain others with them. And they found the stone rolled away from the sepulchre.

And they entered in, and found not the body of the Lord Jesus. And it came to pass, as they were much perplexed thereabout, behold, two men stood by them in shining garments:

And as they were afraid, and bowed down their faces to the earth, they said unto them, Why seek ye the living among the dead?

Taken from the Gospel of Luke, chapter twenty-four

LIFE

But very early on Sunday morning the women went to the tomb, taking the spices they had prepared. They found that the stone had been rolled away from the entrance. So they went in, but they didn't find the body of the Lord Jesus. As they stood there puzzled, two men suddenly appeared to them, clothed in dazzling robes.

The women were terrified and bowed with their faces to the ground. Then the men asked, "Why are you looking among the dead for someone who is alive?"

Taken from the Gospel of Luke, chapter twenty-four

BELIEF

And after eight days again his disciples were within, and Thomas with them: then came Jesus, the doors being shut, and stood in the midst, and said, Peace be unto you.

Then saith he to Thomas, Reach hither thy finger, and behold my hands; and reach hither thy hand, and thrust it into my side: and be not faithless, but believing.

And Thomas answered and said unto him, My Lord and my God.

Jesus saith unto him, Thomas, because thou hast seen me, thou hast believed: blessed are they that have not seen, and yet have believed.

Taken from the Gospel of John, chapter twenty

BELIEF

Eight days later the disciples were together again, and this time Thomas was with them. The doors were locked; but suddenly, as before, Jesus was standing among them. "Peace be with you," he said. Then he said to Thomas, "Put your finger here, and look at my hands. Put your hand into the wound in my side. Don't be faithless any longer. Believe!"

"My Lord and my God!" Thomas exclaimed.

Then Jesus told him, "You believe because you have seen me. Blessed are those who believe without seeing me."

Taken from the Gospel of John, chapter twenty

ETERNITY

Let not your heart be troubled: ye believe in God, believe also in me.

In my Father's house are many mansions: if it were not so, I would have told you. I go to prepare a place for you.

Taken from the Gospel of John, chapter fourteen

ETERNITY

"Don't let your hearts be troubled. Trust in God, and trust also in me. There is more than enough room in my Father's home. If this were not so, would I have told you that I am going to prepare a place for you?"

Taken from the Gospel of John, chapter fourteen

HOME

And I heard a great voice out of heaven saying, Behold, the tabernacle of God is with men, and he will dwell with them, and they shall be his people, and God himself shall be with them, and be their God.

And God shall wipe away all tears from their eyes; and there shall be no more death, neither sorrow, nor crying, neither shall there be any more pain: for the former things are passed away.

Taken from the book of Revelation, chapter twenty-one

HOME

I heard a loud shout from the throne, saying, "Look, God's home is now among his people! He will live with them, and they will be his people. God himself will be with them. He will wipe every tear from their eyes, and there will be no more death or sorrow or crying or pain. All these things are gone forever."

Taken from the book of Revelation, chapter twenty-one

WITNESS

And many other signs truly did Jesus in the presence of his disciples, which are not written in this book:

But these are written, that ye might believe that Jesus is the Christ, the Son of God; and that believing ye might have life through his name.

Taken from the Gospel of John, chapter twenty

WITNESS

The disciples saw Jesus do many other miraculous signs in addition to the ones recorded in this book. But these are written so that you may continue to believe that Jesus is the Messiah, the Son of God, and that by believing in him you will have life by the power of his name.

Taken from the Gospel of John, chapter twenty

THE CHRIST

And he saith unto them, But whom say ye that I am? And Peter answereth and saith unto him, Thou art the Christ.

Taken from the Gospel of Mark, chapter eight

THE CHRIST

Then he asked them, "But who do you say I am?" Peter replied, "You are the Messiah."

Taken from the Gospel of Mark, chapter eight